SPECIAL ★OPS II★

Army Night Stalkers in Action

by Stephen Person

Consultant: Fred Pushies
U.S. Special Operations Forces Adviser

BEARPORT
PUBLISHING

New York, New York

Credits
Cover and Title Page, © U.S. Army photo by Trish Harris, USASOC DCS PAO, © Nathan Derrick; 4, © Mike Durant; 5, © Getty Images; 6, © Getty Images; 7, © PHCM Terry Mitchell; 8, © U.S. Navy photo by Chief Intelligence Specialist Louis Fellerman/Released; 9, © Greg E. Mathieson, SR./MAI /Landov; 10, © 160th Special Operations Aviation Regiment (Airborne); 11, © U.S. Navy photo by Mass Communication Specialist 1st Class Elisandro T. Diaz/Released; 12, © 160th Special Operations Aviation Regiment (Airborne); 13, © Fort Campbell; 14 © Mike Durant; 15L, © Pvt. Jennifer J. Eidson; 15R, © Air Force Staff Sgt. Joshua DeMotts; 16T, © Bettmann/Corbis; 16B, © Bettmann/Corbis; 17, © Courtesy of Igor I. Sikorsky Historical Archives; 18, © J. Alan Elliott/Corbis; 19L, © Wesley Bocxe; 19R, © Stocktrek Images, Inc. / Alamy; 21, © Time & Life Pictures; 22, © Copyright 2001, Columbia Pictures; 23L, © US ARMY RANGERS KRT/Newscom; 23R, © Associated Press; 24, © Reuters; 25T, © United States Army; 25BL, © Associated Press; 26, © T. Mughal/epa/ Corbis; 27, © Christopher Berkey/epa/Corbis; 28TR, © Reuters/Corbis; 28TL, © Courtesy of USASOC; 28B, © DoD photo by Senior Airman Julianne Showalter, U.S. Air Force; 29T, © Chris Keane/Reuters /Landov; 29B, © U.S. Army.

Publisher: Kenn Goin
Editorial Director: Adam Siegel
Creative Director: Spencer Brinker
Design: Debrah Kaiser
Photo Researcher: We Research Pictures, LLC

Library of Congress Cataloging-in-Publication Data

Person, Stephen.
  Army Night Stalkers in action / by Stephen Person ; consultant, Fred Pushies, U.S. SOF Adviser.
    pages cm. — (Special ops II)
  Includes bibliographical references and index.
  Audience: Ages 7–12.
  ISBN-13: 978-1-61772-889-1 (library binding) — ISBN-10: 1-61772-889-6 (library binding)
  1. United States. Army. Special Operations Aviation Regiment (Airborne), 160th—Juvenile literature. 2. Night and all-weather operations (Military aeronautics)—United States—Juvenile literature. I. Pushies, Fred J., 1952– II. Title.
  UA34.S64.P47 2014
  356'.16—dc23

                               2013002388

For more information, write to Bearport Publishing Company, Inc., 45 West 21st Street, Suite 3B, New York, New York 10010. Printed in the United States of America.

10 9 8 7 6 5 4 3 2 1

Contents

Shot Down in Somalia

On October 3, 1993, Chief Warrant Officer Michael Durant was sent on the most dangerous **mission** of his life. A brutal **warlord** named Mohammed Farah Aidid was trying to seize control of Somalia (suh-MAHL-yuh), a country in East Africa. American forces, however, were determined to stop him. Michael was a U.S. Army helicopter pilot. His mission was to fly U.S. **Army Rangers** into the heart of Somalia's capital, Mogadishu (maw-guh-DEE-shoo), so that they could try to capture Aidid.

Michael Durant (far right) with the crew of his Black Hawk

Michael Durant was flying a helicopter called a Black Hawk. This kind of aircraft is specially designed to carry small groups of soldiers to hard-to-reach places.

After Michael flew the soldiers into the city, a fierce battle broke out between the Americans and Aidid's men. Michael was flying just 75 feet (23 m) over the city streets when an enemy **rocket-propelled grenade** (RPG) hit the tail of his helicopter. The aircraft spun wildly out of control and slammed down into the street.

A Black Hawk flying low over the streets of Mogadishu

Somalia is the easternmost country on the mainland of Africa.

5

Captured!

Michael lay in the **cockpit** of his crumpled Black Hawk. He was in terrible pain. Bones in his back and in one of his legs were broken. Bullets were flying all around, and bombs exploded nearby. Two soldiers rushed over to help him out of his helicopter. Before they could rescue him, however, enemy fighters charged up to Michael and grabbed him. Michael Durant was now a prisoner of war.

The remains of Michael's helicopter

Michael's worst fears were coming true. Still, he had known that something like this could happen at any time—and he had accepted the risk. Michael had one of the toughest jobs in the U.S. Army. He was a pilot for a special unit known as the Night Stalkers.

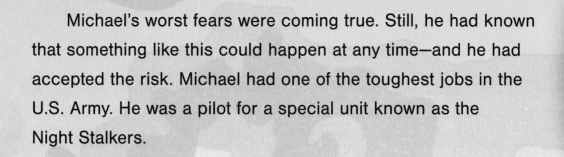

U.S. Marines running from enemy fire in Mogadishu

The battle that Michael fought in became known as the Battle of Mogadishu. Eighteen U.S. soldiers were killed and 84 were wounded, but Aidid was not captured.

NIGHT STALKERS

Night Stalkers

The Army Night Stalkers have a very special job. Using helicopters, they speed into and out of the most dangerous places in the world in order to deliver small groups of **special operations forces**. Often flying behind **enemy lines**, they are called on to help rescue prisoners or capture **terrorists**.

A Night Stalker pilot hovers his MH-47 Chinook just above the deck of a U.S. Navy ship, allowing sailors to climb down.

The official name of the Night Stalkers is the 160th Special Operations Aviation Regiment (Airborne). The Night Stalkers' **motto** is "Night Stalkers Don't Quit!"

As their name suggests, the Night Stalkers often operate at night. Darkness helps them swoop in and surprise the enemy. Not all Night Stalkers are pilots, however. Night Stalker **squads** are made up of expert helicopter pilots like Michael and small groups of highly trained soldiers. Any member of the Army can apply to join the Night Stalkers—but only a select few can do the job.

A Night Stalker crew member prepares to fire from an MH-47G Chinook helicopter.

Tough Training

Tyler DuPont was in for a long and sleepless night. With a team of six other young soldiers, Tyler was holding a 400-pound (181 kg) wooden log. The team had just been ordered to carry the heavy pole on a four-mile (6.4 km) march. After finishing the long trek, the soldiers' next task was to pull a 9,000-pound (4,082 kg) armored truck across the **base**.

Both men and women can be Night Stalkers. These female soldiers train by carrying a heavy log together.

Tyler and the other men were not being punished. They were part of a group of 43 soldiers who wanted to become Night Stalkers. The Army **trainers** were pushing the soldiers hard for one reason. They wanted to find out who was tough enough to become a Night Stalker.

Night Stalkers train at their home base at Fort Campbell, Kentucky.

As part of their training, Night Stalker pilots learn how to drop off and pick up a team of special operations forces quickly.

A Lot to Learn

Tyler got through 12 hours of nonstop lifting and marching. Yet that was just the start of his training. Before becoming Night Stalkers, soldiers must complete a very difficult six-week training course known as Green Platoon. During this time, they learn **navigation** skills and how to give first aid to the wounded. The trainees also practice **combat** skills, including firing weapons and fighting with their bare hands and feet.

Night Stalkers must be experts at using guns and other weapons.

During training, the soldiers practice getting out of a helicopter that is underwater in a swimming pool. This prepares them in case their helicopter is attacked and sinks during combat. Most important of all, the soldiers learn to work as a team during Green Platoon. "You're going to go through some very difficult times," their instructor tells them. "It's teamwork that will get you through."

Of the 43 soldiers in Tyler's group, only 29, including Tyler, successfully completed Green Platoon. All together, there are about 1,800 Night Stalkers in the U.S. Army.

Night Stalkers use this pool to practice getting out of a helicopter that has crashed into the water.

Only the Best

For helicopter pilots like Michael Durant, Green Platoon is just one small part of their training. Michael was already an expert helicopter pilot when he applied to join the Night Stalkers. Still, he faced many months of special pilot training.

Michael Durant in the cockpit of his helicopter

Only the best pilots in the Army are accepted into the Night Stalkers. When Michael applied to this special operations unit, he already had 1,800 hours of flight experience.

Why is this training so important? Night Stalker pilots must fly low to avoid being detected by enemy **radar**. They must also fly at night to avoid being seen. In addition, they're asked to set soldiers down on steep mountains or in the middle of combat zones. These are the most dangerous conditions a pilot can face. Hundreds of hours of practice are needed to prepare a soldier to be a Night Stalker.

Night Stalkers, such as the ones flying this Little Bird helicopter, must be able to get soldiers in and out of dangerous places very quickly.

Night Stalkers need to be experts at flying their helicopters in the dark.

Before the Night Stalkers

When Michael Durant joined the Army in 1978, the Night Stalkers did not exist. The next year, however, 52 Americans were taken **hostage** in Iran. An American mission to rescue the hostages in 1980 failed when three helicopters broke down and two **military** aircraft collided and crashed in the desert. Eight American soldiers were killed.

Americans were held hostage in Iran for 444 days before they were finally released in 1981.

The remains of a helicopter that crashed during the failed rescue mission in Iran

After this failure, Army leaders decided a new special operations unit was needed. The soldiers in the new unit would be specially trained to fly into and out of enemy **territory**. In October 1981, the Army Night Stalkers were formed to take on these very important missions.

Night Stalker pilots carried teams of special operations forces to Grenada in 1983.

The Night Stalkers saw their first combat action on the Caribbean island of Grenada (gri-NAY-duh) in 1983. They flew in American forces that defeated **rebels** who had seized control of the island.

Operation Just Cause

Michael Durant flew his first combat mission, called Operation Just Cause, in 1989. At that time, a **dictator** named Manuel Noriega ruled Panama, a small country in Central America. The Army's task was to **liberate** the people of Panama so that they could choose their own government. Noriega had a powerful military, however, and he was expecting the attack. The Night Stalkers would have to swoop in after dark to surprise the enemy.

U.S. forces helped restore democracy in Panama.

Before taking off on the secret mission, Michael put on his night vision goggles. Flying his Black Hawk just 50 feet (15 m) over the Gulf of Panama, Michael sped toward his target—a Panamanian army base. With bombs exploding all around, he delivered a team of soldiers that was able to capture and take control of the base. The daring work of the Night Stalkers helped remove Noriega from power, making the American mission in Panama a success.

Manuel Noriega

Night vision goggles are one of the Night Stalkers' most important tools. These goggles can gather very small amounts of light and **amplify** it thousands of times, allowing soldiers to see in the dark.

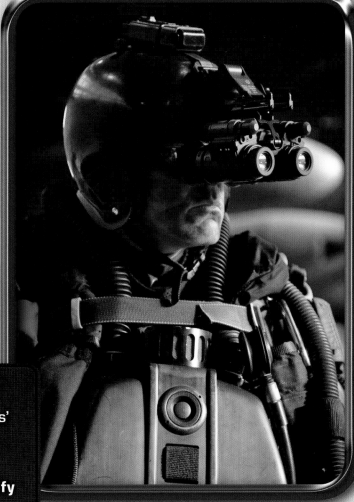

Night vision goggles make everything look green but allow soldiers to see in the dark.

The Dirt Mission

Every Night Stalker mission has different challenges. In 1990, American forces were preparing for Operation Desert Storm. The goal of this mission was to liberate the Arab country of Kuwait (koo-WAYT) from Iraqi invaders. Army leaders wanted to use tanks, but they weren't sure if the heavy tanks would sink in the Iraqi sand. Night Stalker pilots volunteered to find out.

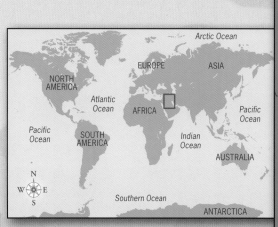

Operation Desert Storm is the name the U.S. government gave to the Persian Gulf War of 1991. Night Stalkers flew many missions during Operation Desert Storm, which lasted from January 17, 1991, to February 28, 1991.

After dark, the Night Stalkers flew deep into enemy territory. They landed their helicopters down in the desert, quickly scooped up samples of the sand, and returned to their base. Army experts tested the sand and found that their tanks would not get stuck in it. Nicknamed "the dirt mission," this daring action helped lead to an American victory in Kuwait the following year.

American tanks were used successfully in Kuwait, thanks in part to the Night Stalkers.

Back in Action

During Operation Desert Storm, one of Michael Durant's tasks was to search for enemy missiles in the desert. When he found one, he destroyed it using guns on his helicopter. The Night Stalkers also flew behind enemy Iraqi lines to rescue injured American special operations forces. Michael's next combat mission was in Somalia in 1993. This was the mission that ended in disaster.

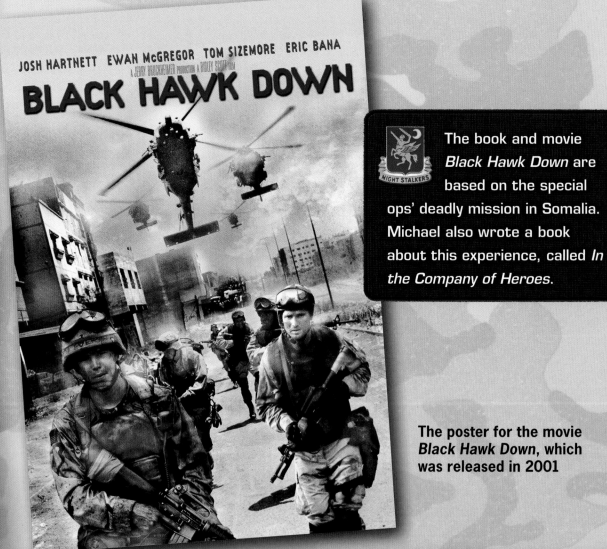

The book and movie *Black Hawk Down* are based on the special ops' deadly mission in Somalia. Michael also wrote a book about this experience, called *In the Company of Heroes*.

The poster for the movie *Black Hawk Down*, which was released in 2001

After being taken prisoner by Somali fighters, Michael became a prisoner of war for 11 days. Finally, the Somalis decided to release him. Back in the United States, Michael faced a long recovery from his wounds. It was more than a year before he was able to return to work. In 1995, Michael climbed back into the cockpit of a Black Hawk. He was a Night Stalker pilot once again.

Michael being carried to an American plane after his release

Michael after his return to the United States

The Missions Continue

Michael retired from the Army in 2001, but the work of the Night Stalkers continues. On September 11, 2001, terrorists **hijacked** four airplanes. They crashed two of them into the Twin Towers of the World Trade Center in New York City. Another plane hit the Pentagon in Virginia, and one crashed into a field near Shanksville, Pennsylvania. Ever since that deadly day, the Night Stalkers have helped lead the worldwide fight against **terrorism**.

Fuel from the planes caught fire after the crashes, causing the Twin Towers to burn and then collapse.

Around 3,000 people died as a result of the terrorist attacks on the United States on September 11, 2001.

The terrorists who attacked the United States were members of a group called Al Qaeda (AHL KAY-duh). Based in Afghanistan, Al Qaeda was supported by the rulers of that country, a group known as the **Taliban**. To prevent future terrorist attacks, American forces entered Afghanistan in October 2001. Night Stalkers flew teams of soldiers into and out of the **rugged** mountains. By the end of the year, American forces helped defeat the Taliban, making it harder for terrorists to use Afghanistan as a base for future attacks.

A Black Hawk lifts off after delivering soldiers to a combat zone in Afghanistan.

Osama bin Laden was the leader of Al Qaeda and planned several terrorist attacks against Americans living and working in different parts of the world.

Protecting Americans

In May 2011, the Night Stalkers flew one of their most important missions. After searching for Osama bin Laden for ten years, American **intelligence agents** discovered that the terrorist leader was hiding in a guarded house in Pakistan. President Barack Obama wanted to send in soldiers to capture him, but this would not be an easy place to reach. It was a job for the Night Stalkers.

The house where bin Laden was hiding

The Night Stalkers flew a team of **Navy SEALs** to bin Laden's house under the cover of darkness. Once there, the SEALs charged into the house and killed bin Laden. Night Stalker pilots then flew the entire force out—without losing a single man. Once again, Night Stalkers had shown the world that "Night Stalkers Don't Quit!"

When the soldiers returned to their base in Kentucky, President Obama came to thank them on behalf of the entire nation.

Army Night Stalkers' Gear

Army Night Stalkers use lots of equipment to carry out their missions. Here is some of the gear they use.

Night vision goggles allow soldiers to carry out missions after dark by amplifying small amounts of light.

Radio headsets allow Night Stalker pilots to talk with crew members and pilots in other helicopters.

Black Hawks are one of three types of helicopters used by Night Stalkers. Black Hawks can transport a fully equipped 11 person squad of soldiers in and out of combat zones very quickly.

Chinook helicopters are bigger than Black Hawks. They can carry more people and larger pieces of equipment, including vehicles.

Little Bird helicopters are designed to attack enemy targets or support troops fighting on the ground.

Glossary

amplify (AM-pluh-fye) to increase in strength

Army Rangers (AR-mee RAYNJ-uhrz) members of the U.S. Army Special Operations Command who have been specially trained for difficult missions

base (BAYSS) the place where soldiers live or operate from

cockpit (KOK-pit) the place at the front of a plane or helicopter where the pilot sits

combat (KOM-bat) fighting between people or armies

dictator (DIK-tay-tur) a person who has complete control over a country and usually runs it unfairly

enemy lines (EN-uh-mee LYENZ) areas of land from where the enemy fights

hijacked (HYE-jakt) illegally took control of an airplane or other vehicle by force

hostage (HOSS-tij) held as prisoners by people who demand money or other things in order to release the prisoners

intelligence agents (in-TEL-uh-juhnss AY-juhnts) people whose job it is to collect and study information about an enemy

liberate (LIB-uh-rayt) to set free

military (MIL-uh-*ter*-ee) having to do with soldiers and the armed forces

mission (MISH-uhn) an important job

motto (MOT-oh) a saying that states what someone believes in

navigation (nav-uh-GAY-shuhn) finding one's way from place to place

Navy SEALs (NAY-vee SEELZ) a small group of sailors in the U.S. Navy who are specially trained to fight at sea, in the air, and on land

radar (RAY-dar) a device that uses radio waves to locate objects such as planes and ships

rebels (REB-uhlz) soldiers who are fighting against a government

rocket-propelled grenade (ROK-it-pruh-PELD gruh-NAYD) a small bomb that is fired by a rocket

rugged (RUHG-id) rough; jagged

special operations forces (SPESH-uhl op-uh-RAY-shuhnz FORSS-iz) groups of highly skilled soldiers in the military; also called special ops

squads (SKWODS) the smallest military units in the army; usually made up of 11 soldiers and a squad leader

Taliban (TAL-uh-ban) a military and political group that ruled Afghanistan from 1996 to 2001

territory (TER-uh-*tor*-ee) an area of land controlled by a country or army

terrorism (TER-ur-*iz*-im) the act of using violence and threats to achieve goals

terrorists (TER-ur-ists) individuals or groups who use violence and terror to get what they want

trainers (TRAYN-urz) people who teach others how to do something

warlord (WOR-lord) a military ruler who has power over a certain area

Bibliography

American Valor: Michael Durant (www.pbs.org/weta/americanvalor/stories/durant_interview2.html)

Durant, Michael J. with Steven Hartov. *In the Company of Heroes.* New York: G.P. Putnam's Sons (2003).

The Official Website of Fort Campbell (www.campbell.army.mil/units/160thSOAR/Pages/160thSOAR.aspx)

Surviving the Cut (DVD). Discovery Channel (2010).

160th SOAR Overview (www.soc.mil/160th/160th%20Overview.html)

Read More

Alvarez, Carlos. *Army Night Stalkers.* Minneapolis, MN: Bellwether Media (2010).

Lunis, Natalie. *The Takedown of Osama bin Laden (Special Ops).* New York: Bearport (2012).

Sandler, Michael. *Army Rangers in Action (Special Ops).* New York: Bearport (2008).

Weiser, Andrea. *U.S. Army Special Operations Command: Night Stalkers Special Operations Aviation.* Mankato, MN: Capstone (2000).

Learn More Online

To learn more about the Army Night Stalkers, visit
www.bearportpublishing.com/SpecialOpsII

Index

About the Author

Stephen Person has written many children's books about history, science, and the environment.